Philosopher's Stone Alchemy Book

STEVEN SCHOOL

DISCLAIMER

Do Not Try This At Home. Not For Consumption. This book does not constitute advice of any type, nor is it intended for any specific person. No warranty is expressed or implied as to the accuracy or completeness of anything presented here.

This book is the black and white edition designed to lower printing costs for those who want to save money. There is a full color edition printed with premium paper. There is also an Electronic Ebook format which is a condensed version for those who prefer to read online, however it has less pages, less images, and less information.

We currently have an alchemy forum called Steven School Alchemy Forum. It is located at Patreon . Com

This book, originally published with Kindle Amazon on 5/10/2023, is not the same as The Philosopher's Stone Book: Alchemy by Steven School.

This new book is the culmination of my fifteen years of experience since I began this journey into the lost hermetic science of alchemy in 2008.

I hope you enjoy this book, I worked hard to learn these things. All those becoming hopelessly lost in the labyrinth, I stayed for the long haul. I wondered, should I let alchemy remain shrouded in mystery? Or should I restore the light of the world which has been kept hidden for centuries. I f you are reading this, you see which choice I made. Let's hope this does not become a banned book.

Steven School, Author.

CONTENTS

Do Not Try This at Home. Not For Consumption.

ACKNOWLEDGMENTS

Michael Sendivogius, The New Chemical Light Alchemy Manuscript , let him consider that this mystery is for wise men and not for fools.

The Emerald Tablets of Thoth Hermes, It's force is above all force, it's power is perfect if it be changed into earth.

Nicholas Flamel Letter To Nephew

George Ripley, Alchemist Manuscripts

Steven School Alchemy YouTube Channel

Alchemy Videos on YouTube

1 EMERALD TABLET OF THOTH HERMES

The Emerald Tablets Hermetic Text is the foundation of the alchemist's art. It dates back thousands of years and is associated with Hermes and the pyramids. Some people theorize there were two emerald tablets instead of one, and that they actually come from Atlantis.

The Emerald Tablet: 'Tis true without lying, certain & most true. That which is below is like that which is above & that which is above is like that which is below to do the miracles of one only thing. And as all things have been & arose from one by the mediation of one: so all things have their birth from this one thing by adaptation. The Sun is its father, the moon its mother, the wind hath carried it in its belly, the earth is its nurse. The father of all perfection in the whole world is here. Its force or power is entire if it be converted into earth. Separate thou the earth from the fire, the subtle from the gross sweetly with great industry. It ascends from the earth to the heaven & again it descends to the earth & receives the force of things superior & inferior. By this means you shall have the glory of the whole world & thereby all obscurity shall fly from you. Its force is above all force. For it vanquishes every subtle thing & penetrates every solid thing. And so was the world created. From this one thing are & do come admirable adaptations whereof the means (or process) is here in this. Hence I am called Hermes Trismegistus, having the three parts of the philosophy of the whole world. That which I have said of the operation of the Sun is accomplished & ended.

Commentary From Michael Sendivogius, The New Chemical Light.

This is the fountain-head of all things terrestrial. Let us illustrate the matter by supposing a glass of water to be set in the middle of a table, round the margin of which are placed little heaps of salt, and of powders of different colors. If the water be poured out, it will run all over the table in divergent rivulets, and will become salt where it touches the salt, red where it dissolves the red powder, and so on. The water does not change the "places," but the several places differentiate the water.

2 ELIXIR OF LIFE ALCHEMY

Alchemy Theory of Steven School, It's impurity removed, The curse is lifted.

The elixir of life in ancient Chinese alchemy symbols is depicted as the white hare on the sphere of the moon.

One of the alchemist main tools, was called an Alembic. It was an ancient and primitive distillation device and predecessor to modern laboratory equipment. The purpose of the Alembic was to "Improve the water.

REVELATION 22:1 NEW INTERNATIONAL VERSION.
Then the angel showed me the river of the water of life, as clear as crystal, flowing from the throne of God and of the Lamb.

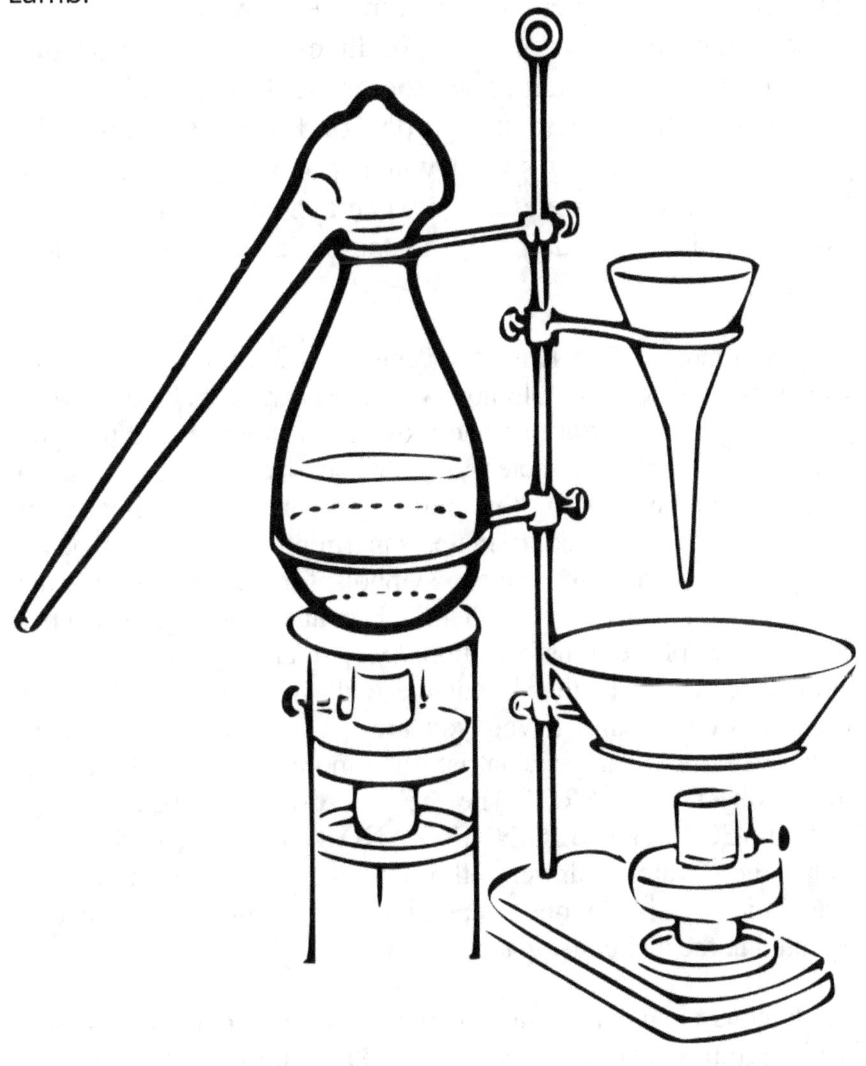

In the history of alchemy, there have been legends of alchemist's staying young and healthy while living extraordinarily long lives. Take Moses for instance, most people do not realize he was an alchemist, but he is recorded as having lived a biblical lifespan of close to one thousand years. Old alchemical manuscripts sometimes depict alchemists having one thousand year life spans. When Adam and Eve were kicked out of the garden of Eden, their immortality was taken away from them by "GOD" and a curse of mortality was placed upon them. This was associated with the fall of man, since we too are reportedly affected by this curse. The path to the garden of Eden was said to be guarded by a flaming sword which points in all directions. Notice the direct correlation between alchemist's and biblical figures, alchemy contains the deepest secrets of the world's religions.

King Solomon of The Knight's Templar was a famous alchemist known for the seal of Solomon which appears to be a star. Most people might leave it at that and move on without second thought, however as with most esoteric occult knowledge there is a much deeper symbolic meaning that most people never see. The seal of Solomon is an inverted triangle, superimposed over a standard triangle. These are the ancient symbols for water and fire, the secret hidden formula of alchemy. Hot and cold equals energy which drives phase transformation. Oxygen and hydrogen unite to form water however this is not the end. When the psychologist asks, 'I want to know, who you are". The reply, "well I exist therefore I am". The psychiatrist once more, "Yes, but I want to know, WHO YOU ARE". The reply, I AM THE ALPHA AND THE OMEGA, THE BEGINNING AND THE END". And so it is with the water, driven through countless evaporations, coagulations, distillations, repetitions of nature's rain cycle, repeated in the alchemist glass.

The famous renaissance era alchemist Paracelsus quoted his belief in his writings that people will never know our sacred art unless they put their hand to the fire, learn the vessels and their uses, perform the experiments. This is a description of the learning process in which the mysteries begin to unfold.

Hermes suggests the venerable stone is hidden in the caverns of the metals. Notice the stalactites and the stalagmites how they grow ever so slowly over the course of time, and the crystals including the metals. Rocks form thrust forth from the earth's crust. Wood becomes petrified or even opalized. Brecciated quartz veins form and sometimes nature fills the cracks with gold. In the writings of Michael Sendivogius New Chemical Light, he associates this with vapors rising through different types of earth. What I am leading up to here is my understanding of what this means. The mineralization process which occurs in the earth. Holy means pure, spirit means water, and thus the holy spirit is pure water. Alchemist's knew this as a trinity, or three levels. The thrice greatest Hermes comes to mind. It begins with the sun, causing the phase transformation to begin. Creating water from oxygen and hydrogen and continuing the rain cycle perpetually. Now "GOD" is the creator of all things yet all things are created by nature. These two are one and the same, watch the stalactites and the stalagmites continue to grow in the caverns of the earth, driven by the same rain cycle which above ground is also causing the trees and plants to grow. Water in the alchemist alembic is separated into three levels of purity driven by heat or fire. That which distills forth over the helm of the distillation vessel is the "most pure" flowing forth from the throne of "GOD" just like pure water forming in the atmosphere before it coagulates and falls to earth. The lower portion of the alembic is called curcurbit, the water here is the "least pure". Resembling that which is found in puddles, lakes, and oceans. As the Archeus of nature rises up in the distillation column it becomes "more pure", or "our air". In the philosophical writings of the early Theologians from the first five centuries that which is "most pure" was called philosophical mercury, (NOT THE ELEMENTAL METAL). That which was more pure, was called "our air", and that which was least pure was called "Sulphur". That which is most high, is associated with "GOD" and is the "most pure" and "GOD" is associated with Immortality. That which is "more pure" is compared to nature's rain cycle and in the world around us represents the very air we breathe, the breath of "GOD" allowing life to be sustained. That which remains in the curcurbit is "least pure" or, the "most impure" and is associated with man who is mortal. Some people believe the leftover impurities in the alchemist glass are the beginning of the metals and may have been used by alchemists for such purposes. Some people call it Ormus white powder gold Old alchemical manuscripts sometimes depict that if we make the wrong choice here, we take death with it. Let's see what the bible says,

PROVERBS 3:16
Long life is in her right hand; in her left hand are riches and honor. Her ways are pleasant ways, and all her paths are peace.

A mysterious white powder was found in the tombs of the Pharaohs, it was associated with the "food of the GOD'S", and the Philosopher's Stone. The Egyptian high priests were alchemists. Sub atomic particles in the water develop through phase transformation which began when hot and cold acting on hydrogen and oxygen caused water to form, the rain cycle then continued the phase transformation until the earth was created, and the earth was void, without form. (GENESIS) This earth, was not yet assigned to any identity. Not yet even a molecule since the nucleus of the atom has not been introduced. The very building blocks of nature which are used to create rocks, stalactites, stalagmites, etc. The cement of the mineralization process. My theory, this is not the pure water of the river of life mentioned in the garden of Eden. Therefore with this hypothesis the impurity is the curse, and when the impurity is removed the curse is lifted. By this I understand my opinion, that when the mineralization process occurs in the human body it is then called, "THE AGING PROCESS". Is "pure water" the elixir of life? Or is there more? Let's see what the bible says.

GENESIS 2:9 ESV.

And out of the ground the Lord God made to spring up every tree that is pleasant to the sight and good for food. The tree of life was in the midst of the garden, and the tree of the knowledge of good and evil.

GENESIS 3:22, 24

Then the Lord God said, "Behold, the man has become like one of us in knowing good and evil. Now, lest he reach out his hand and take also of the tree of life and eat, and live forever—" therefore the Lord God sent him out from the garden of Eden to work the ground from which he was taken. He drove out the man, and at the east of the garden of Eden he placed the cherubim and a flaming sword that turned every way to guard the way to the tree of life.

REVELATION 22:1, & 2 ESV.

Then the angel showed me the river of the water of life, bright as crystal, flowing from the throne of God and of the Lamb through the middle of the street of the city; also, on either side of the river, the tree of life with its twelve kinds of fruit, yielding its fruit each month. The leaves of the tree were for the healing of the nations.

"The leaves of the tree were for the healing of the nations".

EXODUS 32:20 KJV.

And he took the calf which they had made, and

burnt it in the fire, and ground it to powder, and strawed it upon the water, and made the children of Israel drink of it.

Moses anger waxed hot, he was angry with them when he prepared this for mortals.

The Moses alchemy recipe is what the ancient Romans gave the gladiators, Not what he would have prepared for the most high Pharaoh, not fit for his immortal food of the God's.

Moses strangled Pharaoh Ramesis 2 and fled the scene with Pharaoh's army in hot pursuit.

As an alchemist, I envision a scientific equation; fire + Pure Water + Leaves sounds a lot like tea.

Something I would like to say about life force energy. When fruit is on the vine, it is alive and growing. The water inside (holy spirit) is the magnet which attracts life force energy from the air and stores it like a battery. As water comes to the plant, it is first filtered by the dirt. As it travels through the roots and throughout the plant itself, the water is continually being purified since the salts and minerals are either absorbed by the wood, or left behind in the dirt to form rocks. Case in point, the grape vine for instance.

By the time the water has filled the grape it has become purified by the hand of nature, and contains life force energy along with a perfect blend of nutrients for our sustenance. This we find in the garden that was prepared for us. If we consume this fruit fresh picked from the vine, we absorb its life force energy along with hydration and trace nutrients. Once the grapes have been picked, processed, packaged, stored, transported, and finally make it to the grocery store shelf they are alchemically dead. The life force energy is long gone, the flesh has already begun to deteriorate (decompose) contaminating our river of the water. This "food" is no longer fit for consumption and is picked over by scavengers. See how fruit falls to the ground from the tree, when it is past it's prime to be used as food. It now is dead, its path is decomposition to return to the earth from which it came. I need my nutrient fresh, when it is in the upward spiral and vibrant with life force energy to keep me in springtime, even during the winter months when the world around us withers and decays from the frost.

REVELATION 22:1&2 ESV.

Then the angel showed me the river of the water of life, bright as crystal, flowing from the throne of God and of the Lamb through the middle of the street of the city; also, on either side of the river, the tree of life with its twelve kinds of fruit, yielding its fruit each month. The leaves of the tree were for the healing of the nations.

Here we see a monthly harvest for each month, and something extra "GOD" left for us.

GENESIS 1:29 KING JAMES VERSION.

And God said, Behold, I have given you every herb bearing seed, which is upon the face of all the earth, and every tree, in the which is the fruit of a tree yielding seed; to you it shall be for meat.

Over the centuries there have been rumors of Vampirism in the occult world. It was noted centuries ago the life force energy is in the blood. One famous alchemist in history was known as the man who does not die. He was also noted as not aging as time progressed. Of course it could be just speculation. He was also famous for his alchemical preparations. Was he a vampire? Or could he have simply sustained himself with the garden that "GOD" provided for us?

If we study animals in the wild, even whales in the ocean, or dinosaurs for instance. The whales are giant but eat plankton, are they aggressive? I would say no except in the case of the killer whale which is carnivorous. The plant eaters tend to be gentle, yet so vibrant with life force energy they seem electric at times. The meat eaters appear to be stronger and more vicious.

In our world of hamburgers and cooked food, there is no life force energy since it is driven away by heat, also that which is dead is no longer a magnet to attract ethereal energy from the atmosphere. Liquids can store life force energy such as water or even milk. At a colder temperature the amount of life force energy is higher, as heat increases the level of energy is reduced. Apples are a cold weather fruit, if picked fresh from the tree, they can help sustain us during those months when they are ready to harvest. Fresh pack means the apples have been sealed with wax to keep oxygen out, bagged up and sent to supermarkets for long term storage. The last time I bought a bag of store bought apples there was a slightly fermented taste, a scent of pesticide, and the seeds inside were already sprouted trying to grow new apple trees. This is the wrong stage to be considered food in my opinion. Fresh pack keeps it looking fresh longer, similar to embalming a corpse to be put on display. Scavengers eat from the dead. It fills your stomach but has not the electricity of life maintained by the universal spirit. Alchemist's discovered medicines from plants which chemists replaced with synthetic chemicals.

3 WATER STONE ALCHEMY

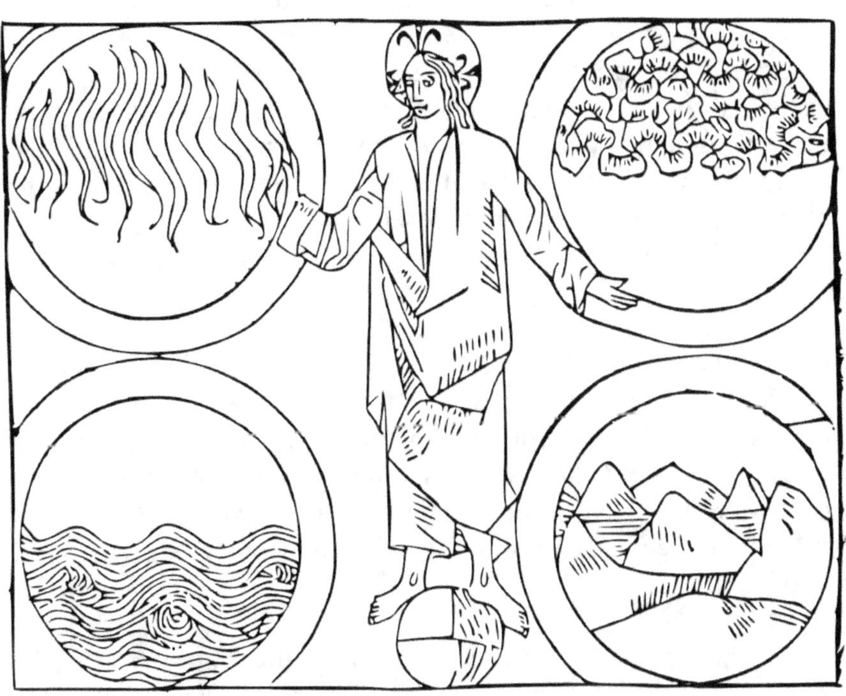

In The New Chemical Light by Michael Sendivogius he writes that water is changed by the place, depending upon what it comes into contact with.

We can see water in various forms of liquid, vapor, ice, "philosophical sulphur" of the alchemist. The Actum Leyden alchemy letter suggests "They took water from the sea" as their matter to be worked upon.

When I look at mountainous gold bearing areas in northern California I see red clay soils containing iron and water. Where gold has been found in Utah I see mineralized ground containing water, and sea salt.

Arizona is said to be home of rich gold deposits such as the lost Dutchman goldmine. But what do I see in Arizona? I see hard mineralized ground, I see the red of iron content, and I see a desert which looks as if it once were the sea floor under an ocean. This would imply to me ground containing sea salt, iron, and water.

In these areas water can sometimes be seen displaying a peacock's tail myriad of colors floating upon the surface. Some people assume this to be associated with chemicals in the soil, and while that could be true I see another possible theory. Perhaps the colorful oil comes from decomposed plant material. Could nature use this substance to color metals and crystals growing in the earths crust?

So the alchemist alembic was used to "IMPROVE THE WATER". The Ourobos in alchemy represents the circle of life. The changing of the seasons. The repetition of nature's rain cycle. The flight of the eagles in the alchemist glass. The medicine wheel of Indian Folklore. Symbolized in alchemy as a serpent eating its own tail. The volatile becomes fixed and the fixed becomes volatile. Solve et Coagula.

The seal of Solomon water and fire compared to the alchemist glass. I see fire (heat) underneath the curcurbit as the catalyst driving the phase transformation, and water inside as the matter or element being worked upon. As water is distilled over the helm the alchemist's called this rising vapor philosophical mercury, (not elemental mercury). More water being continually added to the curcurbit (not the same water that came over the helm as distillate) eventually a material precipitates and the hot liquid begins to turn white. As this process is repeated a white earth forms multiplied in quantity by continuation of this process. This substance is purged by giving out a thick steam or vapor and often resembles wax. At dryness the second type of multiplication begins, which the alchemist's associated with an increase of virtue. The quality of the substance is improved. Here we see the seven steps of alchemy begin.

The Seven Stages of the Alchemical Process; Calcination, Dissolution, Separation, Conjunction, Fermentation, Distillation, and Coagulation.

This is also called the flight of the eagles, the rotations of the alchemist wheel, The second type of multiplication in alchemy where matter is purified and exalted to a higher state of perfection than it was before. A different water was used by the alchemist's for this work, it is the distillate which they called philosophical mercury. (Not The Elemental Metal) but the distilled water which came over the helm. "Philosophical mercury" of seven eagles was said to "sway the moon" which means to dissolve an alchemical substance known by the moon symbol. "Philosophical mercury" of ten eagles (ten multiplications of virtue or repetitions of the seven steps of alchemy). In the writings of Michael Sendivogius he reminds us not to take of the vulgar metals at this point.

In the writings attributed to the alchemist Nicholas Flamel he suggests most people will never make it this far, and of those who do, few if any will ever find the way of proceeding. His writings mention three ingredients which he called sun,moon, and the reason of nature; (philosophical mercury) and not the vulgar metallic element.

A very advance alchemist book came into existence at some time in the past and it was called "LAPIDUS" In Pursuit of Gold.

This book contained commentary on the formulation of the

compound in the alchemist egg. Bridging the gap from the preparation of elements to the composition. But lacking one thing which is also noted in the writings of Michael Sendivogius. The alchemist's up until now have discussed only two philosophical elements being philosophical sulphur, and philosophical mercury (not the vulgar elements of similar names). These are known by certain alchemical symbols which illuminates the third as that of salt. Sendivogius reminds us there are four elements, Lapidus asks for three. We must know then, by what it is ameliorated by.

Alchemist's believed in a secret, hidden element having power to tinge things and to pervade them with color. Alchemical manuscripts suggested this point to be clarified as a gift from "GOD" or the ocular demonstration of a teacher.

Bible Quote
JOHN 12:24 New International Version.

Very truly I tell you, unless a kernel of wheat falls to the ground and dies, it remains only a single seed. But if it dies, it produces many seeds.

And again,
Bible Quote
JOHN 12:24 English Standard Version.

Truly, truly, I say to you, unless a grain of wheat falls into the earth and dies, it remains alone; but if it dies, it bears much fruit.

Michael Sendivogius New Chemical Light.
Eleventh Treatise.

Concerning the practical preparation of our Stone or Tincture by means of our Art.

When you observe at the bottom ashes of a brown color, while the water is almost red, you should open the vessel and dip a feather into it. With this feather smear a morsel of iron, and if it becomes tinged, pour into the vessel as much of a certain water (which we will describe hereafter) as there is of crude air which has entered in, and then again subject it to coction over the same fire, until it colors the feather again. Further than this my experience does not go. The water I have mentioned is the menstruum of the world from the sphere of the Moon and so carefully rectified that it has power to calcine the Sun.

Hermes Vessel of Nature has thus been illuminated. The work of the sun and moon is ended. As a thing begins, and so it ends. I am the Alpha and the Omega, the beginning and the end. Thrice Greatest Hermes.

4 METAL ACETATE PATH

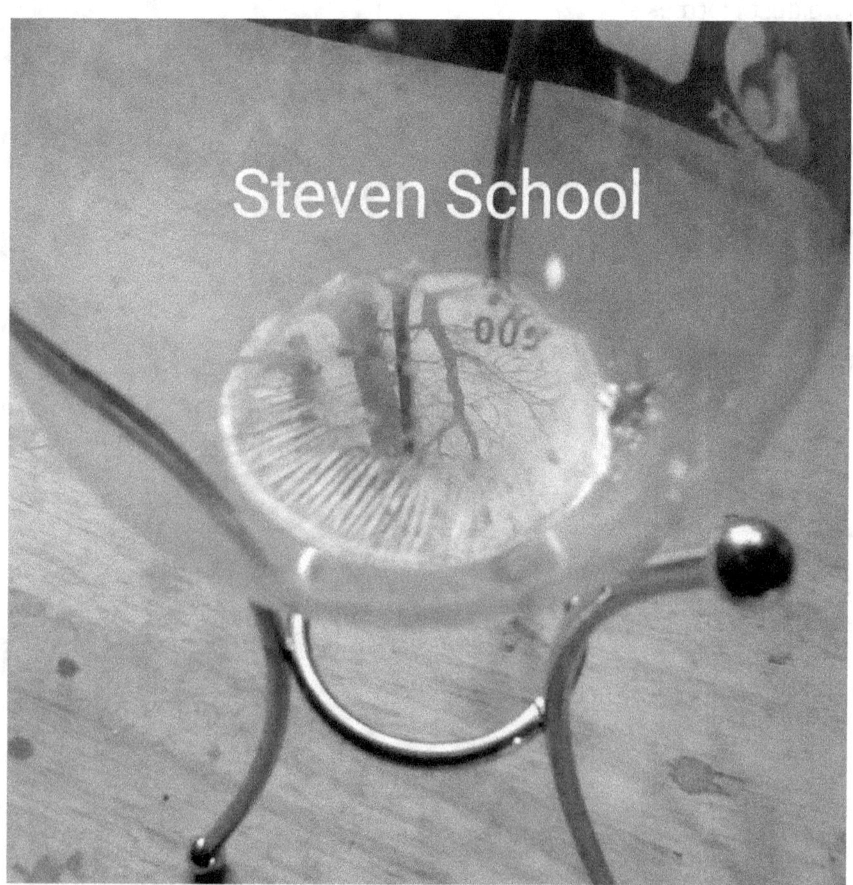

Peacock's tail Cauda Pavonis Wet Path Alchemy Acetate Path.

The metal acetate path of alchemy was made famous by the alchemist George Ripley author of the Ripley Scroll and the bosom book of Ripley. It was also highlighted in the works of Theophrastus Paracelsus who gave a brief overview speaking of that vinegar being colored yellow. The ancient Romans figured out long ago that rocks could be dissolved with vinegar. Notice how the name Paracelsus sounds similar to Peracetic.

The basic idea of the metal acetate path of alchemy revolves around iron and sulfur. Solve et Coagula but also multiplication of said matter. Alchemist's tried the experiments myriad different ways with different results in order to solve the puzzle. It has been said that this is all a work to the white and the red, and that these are the two substances prepared for conjunction in this work. Join the red man to the white wife was one of the most popular alchemical motto's concerning this union of white earth and fiery red oil. In the writings of John Pontanus concerning the secret book of Artephius he suggests that the "whole matter" is changed by the action of the "water" alone. Alchemical symbolism of the green lion devouring the sun with seven stars on his back and the red drops flow. The seven stars represent the seven planetary metals of alchemy which the green lion has power to dissolve. Images of the green lion devouring the sun in alchemy depicts a secret, it means the black sun known to the alchemist.

The way the metal acetate path of alchemy is written out in Ripley's bosom book is not exactly direct and to the point. It does show that he invested considerable time in his experiments trying them in different ways. I can visualize what he was doing by his words because I also went through this labyrinth of performing experiments and examining the results in order to find the way. Even the way Paracelsus spoke of this work was rather confusing. I shall simplify this matter by describing the basic framework of it without going so deep as to further confuse the issue. The matter being well crushed in a suitable mortar and pestle as fine as the painters grind the colors, was then placed into a suitable extraction vessel, (Glass Jar) and the prepared menstruum added. The top closed with the seal of Hermes which is not a seal at all but a breathable dust cover. The vinegar being colored yellow was poured off or decanted and new menstruum added to the material. This process was repeated until nothing more extracts. All the yellow vinegar was saved and called our chaos. It contains our white "earth", not yet pure.

The leftover capuut mortuary in the glass was then roasted and calcined in a reverberatory furnace or athanor until it had gone through the color changes of the peacock's tail and the purple glory to become the final fixed red no longer affected by fire. Upon cooling this material was placed into another jar and fresh menstruum added to it. This jar is also called chaos but is left undisturbed. Over time it will dissolve and extract, leading to a separation of layers wherein the red oil floats atop. Alchemist's carefully scooped off the "top water" without disturbing the sediment which gave them the fiery red oil called "dragons blood" which is our red lion and our secret red mercury, not elemental mercury. The sediment contains the fixed centric salt.

Some alchemist's believed the yellow vinegar could be processed the same way, while other's examined the matter with myriad experiments which I will explain.

If the yellow vinegar is placed in a distillation vessel and heat is applied, we get what alchemist's called vitrification. It appears to me what is note able here is that oxygen is basically sealed out and the matter "cooked" in our water. The outcome is an oily saffron colored metallic crystalline mass which seems to be unaffected by heat and stains everything it touches with oily golden color. Some of the old alchemy manuscripts suggested this out come was undesirable but could be saved by redissolving the substance in fresh menstruum. I theorize we must be careful with heat and oxygen to prevent formation of metals until the immature substance is submerged in molten metal to be transmuted, and then let the reaction occur.

If the yellow vinegar is evaporated outside in a large open pot over an electric hot plate on low to moderate heat, reducing the heat as we approach dryness, we get a green acetate which I call my green lion. Alchemist's believed this substance will dissolve metals and place them back into the crystal growing stage. Alchemist's believed the metals resolve in this "water" because they supposedly originally were this "water". Such evaporations like this are not done inside due to fumes and the formation of a strange green mold which seems to develop on everything the vapor touches. Fume hoods, personal protective equipment, laboratory standards etc.

If, during the evaporation of this green lion too much heat is used and we burn the matter, a steam arises, then a white fume issues forth, the remaining material being calcined into a red powder which in alchemy would be called a sulphur element due to its nature. It's appearance is that of a dry red powder that seems to be unaffected by heat.

If we properly receive this green lion without burning its flowers nor destroying its green color we can very carefully dry it in warm sunlight then we can seal it in airtight glass so it does not revert to liquid. It burns very easily, driving out the volatile natures.

Once we have this green lion carefully prepared we can distill it gently in a borosilicate glass retort and it becomes black like molten liquid pitch, bubbling like unto the eyes of fishes. Keeping it thus in fusion, a clear distillate comes over the helm which in alchemy would be labeled philosophical mercury, (not elemental mercury). It is stoppled close and is a dissolving water.

From here there are two possible ways to proceed. One is a dry path experiment, and the other wet.

Once the clear distillate has come over the helm of the distillation vessel and is stoppled close, a new receiver or receptacle is attached to the distillation apparatus. I always make a loose connection here and wrap it with plastic wrap to avoid pressure expansion cracking the glass. The heat is raised by degrees and a volatile white substance dry distills from the black earth. It adheres to the upper walls and neck of the retort like unto a white waxy salt, or the congelation of a frosty vapor. With this method alchemist's were usually faced with the possibility of having to break the retort. This matter can be saved by dissolving everything with vinegar and saving the glass.

The wet method. Reaching into the retort with a thin wooden stick made for shishkabobs, I broke up the black earth and dumped it out into a beaker. This material can be stored in sealed glass to keep it clean and dry. To process it, I placed it in a beaker with white vinegar and set it on a warm hotplate. I can also flush out the retort with vinegar and add it to the beaker. (store bought white vinegar 5% acidity, 95% distilled water). I stirred the hot liquid solution until everything soluble was dissolved and then filtered it. The remaining solution was then further evaporated to a super saturated saline solution and covered with a coffee filter. This beaker was allowed to sit undisturbed overnight on the counter at room temperature and a white waxy looking material formed. The filter was thrown away.

A faster way to the white substance. I took several large glass pickle jars washed and dried. I ground iron pyrite crystals in mortar and pestle by hand. I prepared these jars by adding quantities of iron pyrite along with the two part menstruum I had developed through research. Composed of white vinegar and hydrogen peroxide it is called peracetic acid. It is believed to have power to dissolve soft metals gently. This can be a dangerous substance. I covered the top of the jars with coffee filters held in place by rubber bands. This keeps dust and insects out but allows expanding gases to escape without cracking the glass. These jars were stored in a well ventilated area undisturbed for long term. As the dissolution occurs and the matter is left undisturbed we see the separation of layers in the glass. If we do not decant the solution and let the jars evaporate, the white substance is found adhering to the sides of the glass, having separated itself from the earth below. This material appears to be composed of the white substance along with a yellow which I call oil.

Some alchemist's believed in preparing two glasses, one for the yellow vinegar experiment (green lion) and the other for the red. (In the previously described fashion). These jars left undisturbed to dissolve, extract and form a separation of layers. The alchemist's carefully scooped off the top water without disturbing the sediment. A spoon works for this. The yellow vinegar is used to do the imbibitions in an empty flask evaporating and forming the earth. The process then being repeated with the red lion oil to dissolve, coagulate, and "multiply" the first substance.

Crystal formation was also noted during these experiments.

Black Sun Alchemy Symbols Black White Red.

Dry Path Alchemy Experiment Image With Iron And Sulfur.

5 ANIMAL STONE ALCHEMY

Alchemist's such as Michael Sendivogius and Theophrastus Paracelsus were said to have practiced experiments in the animal realm of alchemy which was also made famous by Hennig Brandt when he found phosphorus. This type of alchemy was republicized by the book of Aquarius and developed a large following in the book of Aquarius forum which seemed to focus upon one matter as the substance. Look inside yourself they said. The power is in you.

My experience with the animal realm of alchemy began with old mason jars with the glass lids. I removed the rubber seals since the seal of Hermes is not a perfect seal and the idea was to keep dust and insects out of the experiment. The allowance of expanding gases to escape prevents the cracking of the glass, and the small exposure to oxygen allows the putrefaction to occur.

Forty days (a philosophical month) the matter well putrefied I set up a hotplate, and a sand bath. Using a borosilicate glass retort I distilled the top ten percent of the most volatile water and stoppled it in a flask. The remaining material was transported outside and evaporated to dryness then calcined until no more smoke, fume, or stench issued forth and I was left with a black earth. I placed this black earth into a flask in a low heat sand bath and connected a retort which I filled with the clear distillate. The matter began to distill ever so gently over the helm at the temperature of a hatching chicken, gently wetting the parched dry earth which I had calcined. In three days time a white stone had formed in the center atop the black earth.

In the 1800's a book was said to have been published by a young woman with permission of her father who had not bothered to read the manuscript first. The book began selling many copies which finally peaked the mans interest and so he decided to actually read it. The book was about alchemy and disclosed secrets of the art kept hidden in their family for generations away from public view. After reading the book the father was not happy and ordered the printing stopped. He then went around buying up all the copies of the book which he burned, thinking that he had rounded up every last one. Somehow at least one copy must have survived, perhaps the printer had kept a proof. In later years the book resurfaced in print again. Secrets of alchemy were said to have been in this book which someone did not want published. It was a very long winded book containing the usual wording that makes you really have to think what they were alluding to.

There were however gems buried deep within the pages of this book. My understanding of the material after reading it, is that it focused upon the animal realm of alchemy which holds deep secrets in this art. After distilling all of those written words, I can give a condensed version of what was important. It spoke of a matter in alchemy that was partially illuminated in a modern publication called the book of Aquarius. The older work seemed to unlock the missing pieces of the puzzle. It spoke not so much of recipes temperatures, laboratory procedures or time frames, but focused instead upon the ingredients or matter to be taken in hand for the particular work that was its focus. As I have already indicated, the focus of this alchemy book was upon the animal stone. It spoke of the matter itself, and a secret water of an ethereal nature, a vital and living water so to speak. The first matter, as illuminated spoke of the corporeal body. An earthy misty body to be focused upon as the subject matter. The book indicated this substance, when it becomes manifest in nature clings to the earth. It is known by all but considered of little worth. Despised and cast out into the street, trodden underfoot. In its first efflorescence it is considered black, the misty corporeal body or earth. This substance when prepared by nature and left undisturbed without the laying on of hands has been known to undergo changes which alchemists noted by a series of colors. The first main color change seen was white. The matter became as a dry white earth. After this, transformation continued until the substance took on the appearance of a dry red powder. A red Adamic earth. Like a red powder.

The red powder was only part of the story. We shall now remind the reader that this substance or material was said to be ameliorated by a second substance which has been described as a secret water. A water known to the alchemist. This second substance or "water" is akin to the first matter as if to say its shadow, or somehow related to it. The imbibitions of the living water resurrect the dead, corporeal body from the sepulcher. Just as Jesus had arisen from the tomb.

The secrets of alchemy in the animal realm run deep. Before we continue in that direction let us look at some bible quotes about the red Adamic earth.

1 Corinthians 15:47. The first man is of the earth, earthy. He was formed out of the earth, (Genesis 2:7) and the word there used signifies red earth.

What does the red "Adamic earth" mean?
A well known Hebrew name Adam means son of the red earth. Its meaning comes from the Hebrew word Adamah meaning earth, from which Adam is said to be formed.

The animal realm of the ancient hermetic science of alchemy runs much deeper that just the animal stone. Alchemists made supplements such as egg shell bhasma said to regrow teeth.

In the art of distillation by John French he illuminates the salt volatile as being beneficial for skin afflictions. Common sense dictates that this would not be for cuts scrapes or burns, but perhaps other issues like psoriasis or eczema.

If you have experience with book of Aquarius type alchemy then you know the salt volatile as being the most volatile portion of the putrefied liquid distillate, (top ten percent) and the volatile salt which can be gathered in an Aludel. (Alchemist glass device).

In food alchemy with cooking, there is what is called bone soup. Ribs are added to a pot of water along with other basic soup or stew ingredients and then cooked. The hot water breaks down the bone marrow and extracts from it. This is supposed to help with leaky gut syndrome or damage to the stomach lining. The creation of soup stock, or soup base, comes from boiling bones to get the marrow. Beef bones were used to make beef soup stock, chicken bones for chicken soup stock, and fish bones for fish soup stock. Some people would bake the bones first in an oven before boiling them to help break down the calcium. Garlic and oregano are also used in cooking, they have antibacterial, antiviral and antiparasitic qualities, which means they are natural antibiotics. Bones, are in the animal realm of alchemy and were used to make bone meal, a basis of food. We are still in animal realm alchemy.

Flight of eagles, multiplication in alchemy. Exaltation or purification of matter.

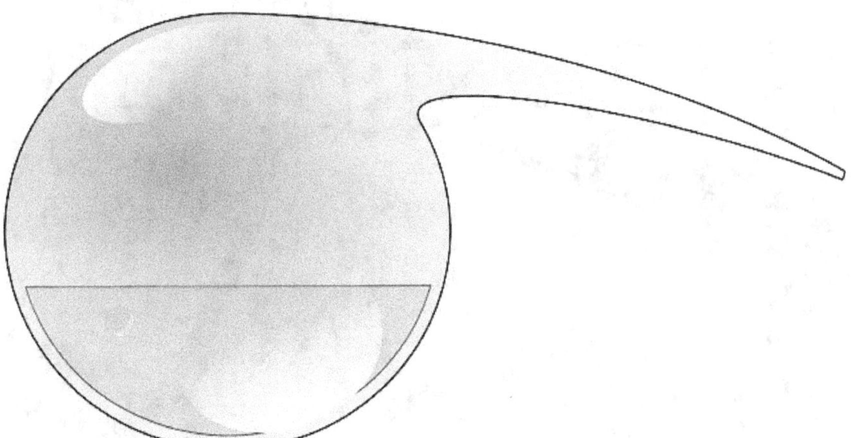

The alchemist glass retort, is a basic alchemist tool for laboratory distillation. Matter is placed into the glass and distilled over the helm. At dryness we are left with an earth in the glass which is then calcined directly in the retort until no more smoke, fume, or smell arises. This earth is now the capuut mortuary or our earth, the body, which is dead. The distilled liquid is then returned to the parched earth and this is called imbibition. This constitutes one flight of the eagle or one turn of the alchemist wheel. This process purifies the matter. We now proceed to distill the liquid a second time, at dryness the earth is calcined and then the water returned to the parched earth completing a second turn of the alchemist wheel. With each repetition of this cycle, the matter becomes more pure, and a fiery dissolving water. Seven flights of the eagle is said to sway the moon. Ten flights of the eagles is said to have power to calcine the sun. This means to dissolve metal or other substances. We will illuminate the black sun in this book. The water in this work is called "philosophical mercury" which is not elemental mercury.

Mercury of ten eagles in the animal realm means putrefied ethereal "water" distilled ten times, which has nothing to do with elemental mercury metal. They are not the same thing. (This differs from the secret water stone of Hermes). "Mercury" represents the water element or liquid. Not elemental mercury metal.

Steven School Alchemy YouTube Channel

6 SECRETS OF THE PHILOSOPHER'S STONE

Hermes Philosopher's Stone was said to be made from a legendary substance called Carmot.

This section is about secrets of alchemy, by Steven School.

The ancient Egyptian obelisk carved with hieroglyphs symbolizes the tree of life rising up into eternity. Hermetic alchemy science revolved around water, fire, and the tree of life. (A work of Hermes). This type of alchemy was called the secret water stone of the wise,or the sophick hydrolith. The water stone. Alchemical symbolism often depicts two waters flowing into the cup.

Michael Sendivogius illuminates the above mentioned tree in The New Chemical Light Alchemy Manuscript.

The Black sun in alchemy is associated with the metal iron. It is calcined to remove any oils which may have been applied to the metal to prevent rust. The alchemist secret key to unlock the metal is the alchemy formula solve et coagula which means dissolve and coagulate. The alchemist secret water imbibed into the substance caused color changes to occur, black white red. The alchemist's had aninterest in iron pyrite since they were working with the unification of iron and sulfur by a dry path method involving heat in which oxygen had to be sealed out of the equation, and also a wet path which required dissolution and coagulation instead of heat. This type of early modern alchemy falls into the category of the metal acetate path and was practised by such alchemist's as George Ripley, and Theophrastus Paracelsus. This is not the same as the work of Hermes or Michael Sendivogius. The metal acetate path of alchemy is said to be a work to two substances, one white and the other red. After unification and three multiplications it is said to create a red crystal composed of three parts of the fiery red oil to one part of the white earth.

Animal Realm Alchemy was promoted in modern times by the book of Aquarius. Medieval renaissance era alchemist's Michael Sendivogius and Theophrastus Paracelsus also performed public demonstrations utilizing this type of alchemy but they were ridiculed and harassed. It is said in alchemy "The power is in you", and so it is. Two matters the alchemist takes in hand and these are called sun and moon. One is the corporeal body or our "earth" the other is a secret water used for performing the imbibitions upon said "earth". Alchemist's made niter beds and sometimes even just dug around old outhouses and leached the soil. The material acquired from the soil was a white salt. The corporeal body is said to undergo color changes first white, and then red. This work is not the same as the acetate path, or a work of Hermes.

Why was the philosopher's stone of alchemy said to require being wrapped in wax?

Wax was commonly used by alchemists making balms, salves and creams from essential oils. It was also sometimes used as an ingredient in soap making. The acetate path alchemist George Ripley suggested philosopher's Stones were wrapped in wax partly due to their oily nature.

The oils of the metals are a part of alchemy just like the oils of plants and herbs. There is however more to it than just this, bees wax was used as a fluxing agent in primitive metallurgy and some experiments are affected by the presence of oxygen. A "philosopher's stone" wrapped in wax, could theoretically keep out the oxygen until the material is submerged under the surface of the molten metal being "transmuted". The word pyramid, means "fire in the middle". Not fire on top.

Alchemists who dropped their transmutation powder onto molten metal did not leave it to sit there. They "INSTANTLY" plunged it under the surface with a rod and began stirring. A lid can be placed upon the crucible to extinguish flames by sealing out oxygen.

This is alchemy in the realm of metallurgy, not for consumption, and not to be confused with animal realm alchemy, or a work of Hermes. This type of work is not the same as the secret water stone of the wise. Do not try this at home.

I reacted Iron pyrite with nitric acid which I decanted as a brown root beer colored liquid and precipitated a substance looking like white wax through evaporation. Alchemy experiment with Iron pyrite and nitric acid by Steven School.

Alchemist Secret "Red Mercury" Iron Pyrite Red Lion Acetate Path.

In this experiment I had extracted Iron pyrite many times with peracetic acid to remove the green lion acetate and then calcined the left over material. As I roasted the Iron pyrite it displayed colors of the peacock's tail including blue and purple among others which eventually resulted in a final fixed red or "sulfur incombustible" The red material was then separated into two portions and one was placed back into a jar for a wet path alchemy experiment. I added more of the menstruum vinegar and peroxide and covered the top of the jar with plastic wrap. I left the jar undisturbed for several months as extraction and separation occurred. I carefully removed the plastic wrap without disturbing the sediment or moving the jar. Using a spoon I very carefully scooped the red oil from the surface of the top water. (not for consumption). The fiery red oil is called dragons blood and "RED MERCURY", which is not elemental metallic mercury.

Old alchemy manuscripts such as Ripley's bosom book on the metal acetate path of alchemy suggest the red oil is used to imbibe the white material in a series of three imbibitions which are called multiplications. Ripley suggested one part red oil to one part white substance for each turn of the wheel using a water bath to dissolve and coagulate. This is supposed to lead to the creation of a red glass like crystal. It is not the same as a work of Hermes or the animal stone, it is also not the water stone of the wise. This work lies in the realm of metallic alchemy and is a toxic poison. It seems ridiculous to have to mention that but over the centuries many would be alchemists died from drinking their experiments. Alchemists call the red oil gold and affix the sun symbol, the white earth is symbolized by the moon. Each realm of alchemy can use the basic symbols but they are not food.

We have discussed the wet path of alchemy in the metal acetate work and seen how alchemist's improved it with the development of nitric acid. Much faster than old methods using vinegar or even peracetic acid.

In the alchemical writings of Paracelsus he obviously performed myriad experiments however from his coded words and using eyes of experience it appears that he did use the nitric acid method (among others) and from my own experience I see it this way, he took iron pyrite and ground it to powder, placed it into a glass retort and distilled it with nitric acid, calling the earthly body the white wife and the distillate the red man. I believe the flights of the eagles were then performed returning the distilled nitric acid back to the earthy material in the retort. Ten flights of the eagles should have dissolved everything and created a "stone" from the red man and the white wife.

The black sun in alchemy is iron, black for its color and its first treatment in the alchemical process is calcination to remove any impurities such as oils. It is also called the black stage of alchemy because it is black, but it is called the black sun because alchemists united it with sulfur. This is why they worked upon Iron pyrite, iron and sulfur are already together in the mineral substance.

In my dry path of alchemy I used Iron pyrite which I ground to powder in a mortar and pestle. I washed the material clean many times with white vinegar and hydrogen peroxide. I then calcined the pyrite in my Athanor alchemist furnace for three days until it had gone through all the colors of the peacock's tail resulting in the final fixed red. I used a cast iron pot with a wooden handle and an iron lid. The quantity of pyrite mostly filled the pot so there was only a small gap between the lid and the roasted material.

I placed this pot on an electric hotplate and turned the heat up as high as it would go. When full temperature was reached, I began casting flowers of sulfur onto the hot iron pyrite. I noticed that in the presence of oxygen the sulfur will burst into flame which was undesirable. I discovered that by using the cast iron lid as a tool, I could solve this problem. I lifted the hot lid using a glove and a tool, cast the sulfur onto the iron pyrite and quickly replaced the lid to seal out the air. If the sulfur did ignite it quickly burned up the oxygen in that small space and flames were extinguished. This was the secret I learned by manual experience to unite iron and sulfur, multiplying the first substance with the second, the burning of the sulfur avoided. Once I had developed this process, upon the sulfur hitting the hot metal it was changed into a solid red mass hard as stone which I began to grind to a red powder. The material was also stuck to the iron pot and I was not able to separate the two. If I recreate the experiment I will probably use a sledge hammer to break the pot next time. Using tools to break up the red stone into smaller stones to work in an iron or steel mortar and pestle. This material is too hard to grind in a glass mortar and pestle. Medieval alchemists would use vinegar to soften up the red mass.

Green lion alchemy book by Steven School.

Alchemy and the Green Lion Book Cover Image.

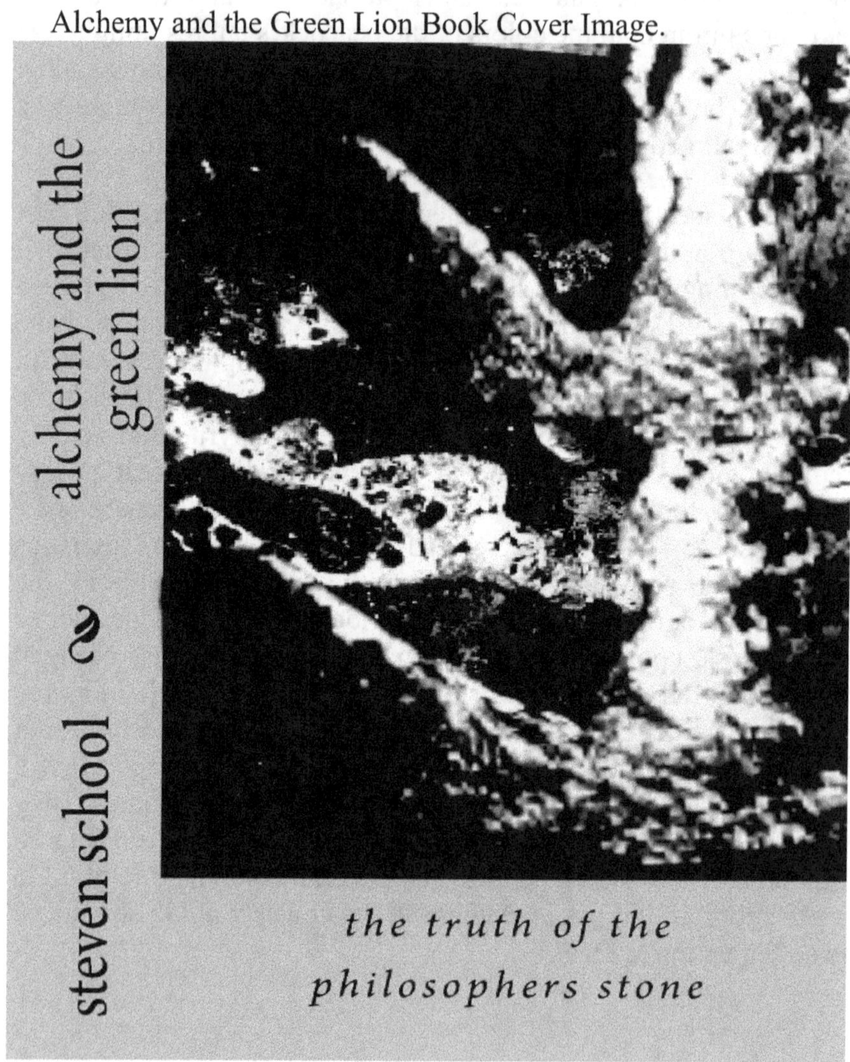

My first alchemy publication.

Some of my transmutation experiments involved casting flowers of sulfur onto molten lead, along with uniting sulfur to iron and grinding it to powder, which was then wrapped in hammered lead as an enclosed ball before casting on molten lead. These were old primitive experiments that I did long ago. Back then I had roughly four years of experience with alchemy. I am now at the fifteen year mark and would do things a little differently.

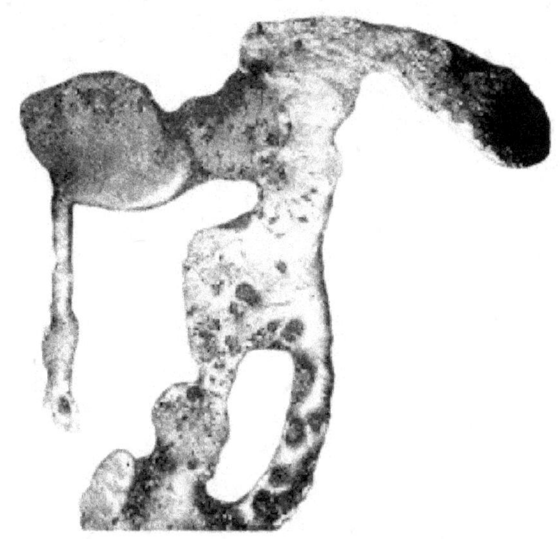

Early transmutation attempted experiment by Steven School. Casting flowers of sulfur on molten lead.

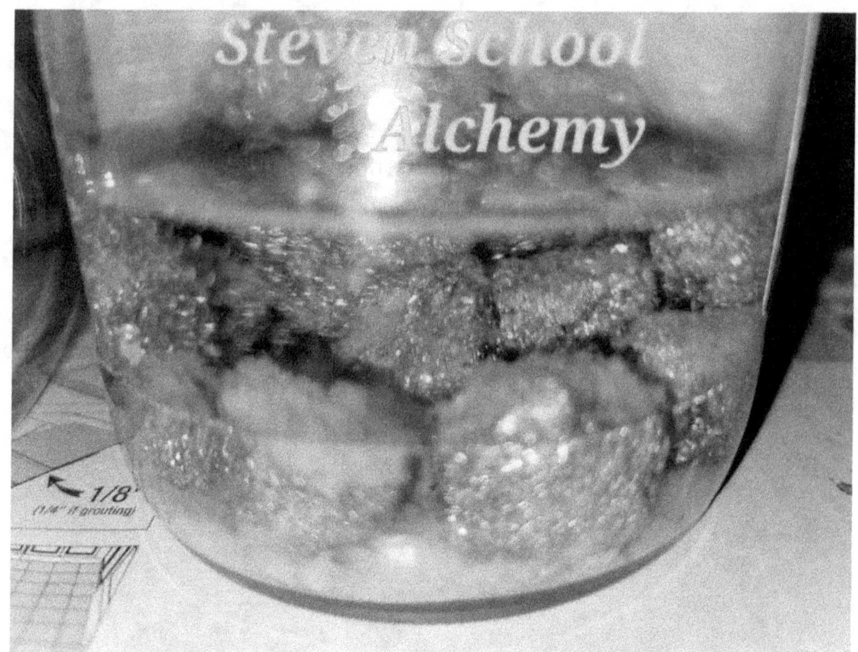

Acetate path alchemy aka wet path. Extraction of Iron pyrite with peracetic acid. Alchemy of Steven School. Do not try this at home.

If you have followed my works in alchemy then you may recall the story of the book of three words in which I discovered an old science book in a thrift store by accident. This book had a short section on alchemy and the thing that caught my attention were three words which I had mentioned on YouTube. Some people asked me for the secret of the three words. I had compared these words to the Actum Leyden Alchemy letters and made experiments based on the information which were highlighted in some of my YouTube videos. People indicated they wanted to know just exactly what these three words were. The answer to the question is salt, vinegar and copper. Sea salt and white vinegar are interesting as an agent to work upon copper metal. This is interesting because my research indicates nature uses sea salt as a fluxing agent when rubies are formed naturally in the earth's crust. By adding vinegar, it might have a little more dissolving power than ordinary seawater, it also would be much easier to prepare. In my research on mineral content of gold bearing soils I find sea salt present and the crystal structure seems to match that of gold crystals and also fluorite. I understand here that sea salt may act upon matter, and play a role in the formation of crystals, metals, and gemstones in the earths crust. Solve Et Coagula. Just imagine what might occur if I place sea salt, vinegar, and copper metal into my alchemist glass retort and perform ten flights of the eagle. I can envision dissolution and crystal growing with colors provided from the metal. Such crystallization that perhaps I could finish exalting by using heat in an oven the same way that sunset rubies are improved in the laboratory. Sea salt and the salt of the metal forming a new crystal of higher quality and colored perfectly by the hand of nature as it is extracted from the metal. This might be an easy way to the creation of alchemical gemstones in the alchemist laboratory.

By starting with substances such as sea salt and vinegar, alchemist's experiments led to the discovery of stronger, more powerful acids which combined with metallurgy, expedited their alchemical experiments in the realm of the metals.

The experiments of the alchemist's laid the blessed cornerstone for the emergence of modern science and chemistry, which of course has strayed from the path of the ancients. The invention of such things as the 17th century short barreled musket grenade launcher must have been fun as hell, but with such inventions also came the rise of evil. Alchemist's discovered that medicines came from plants in the garden that was built for us. Chemists synthesized medicines by reproducing them with chemicals which are not the same thing and do not reach the same outcome. At one time bodies created what was needed from sunlight, pure water, and vitamin c.

The alchemist's dream. I posted a brief article on the community tab of my YouTube channel about the alchemist dream I had, people mentioned in the comments they would like to know more information. I shall place that information here so we can see the importance of it. There have been times in my life when I had questions that were answered in my dreams. This has happened a few times but only about major key issues of which there have been three. The one that concerns this book however is the alchemist's dream.

I had gone to bed and drifted off into a deep sleep. I began to dream that I was hiking in a rugged mountainous rocky terrain sparsely forested with trees. As I climbed upward and forward I found a pocket of brilliantly colored translucent crystals displaying all the myriad colors of the peacock's tail. I gathered them up knowing there was some importance here and wondered from whence they had come. As I continued my astral journey I soon discovered the source of these crystals. It was a large old pine tree which quite obviously had been injured. As I examined the trees wounds I found the source of the crystals which had evolved from the tree sap. After this I took more of an interest in this tree in the midst of the garden.

The red stone or oil that is on the cover of some of my older alchemy books such as alchemy survival guide, and alchemy and the ravens head secret of the red mercury. The work that I did which resulted in the aforementioned images. I took small gold nuggets, placer gold from rivers. I pounded the gold nuggets flat and thin, and then washed them clean with alcohol. I extracted the green lion acetate from Iron pyrite and distilled it in a glass retort to receive the clear distillate which I at that time had called the blood of the green lion. I distilled this liquid into a borosilicate round flask in which I placed one gold nugget beaten thin and washed, I then stoppled this with a glass stopper. I filled a metal pot with sand to create a sand bath and buried in it this alchemist "egg" I placed it atop a wood burning stove and built a fire. Reactions occurred which seemed to be driven by heat. The gold seemed to begin dissolving or perhaps its essence was simply extracted from it. Crystallization appeared visually and the water became colored. Hues of yellow, orange, and then blood red liquid as the gold turned black. When the heat was too high the glass stopper popped out and I reinstalled it. The heat appeared to drive the dissolution and the coagulation along with the change in colors. In heat the substance now looked like a crystal, however when the heat was removed or reduced, the "red crystal" would revert to what appeared to be a blood red "oil" which must be in alchemy, the oil of gold. It looks much like the dragons blood extracted from calcined pyrite which alchemist's call pure gold.   See book cover images next.

SOPHICK HYDROLITH ALCHEMY

ALCHEMY EGG UPDATE
1-15-2023

STEVEN SCHOOL ALCHEMY
YOUTUBE CHANNEL

imgflip.com

SECRET WATER STONE OF THE WISE

The water stone in the ancient hermetic science of alchemy is illuminated in the new chemical light alchemist manuscript by Michael Sendivogius. He credits this type of alchemy to Hermes as does Paracelsus in his works. Together they both suggest it to be different from the myriad works of early modern alchemist's who came after them. This work is summarized by the seal of Solomon which is the ancient symbol for water and fire shown as a star. This stone came in two forms, one white and the other red. The red stone is made in the vessel of nature as outlined in this book without the laying on of hands, nature doing the work. One matter one vessel the alchemist only sets the proper conditions etc. It is made from water, but the water is changed by the place as Sendivogius has told us. Through so many circulations until it appears ready to the hand. The "white stone" is prepared using water, fire, and the alchemist distillation retort. This is symbolized by the Ourobos in alchemy. Water is placed into the alchemist distillation vessel and heat is applied. The water distills over the helm and is discarded. New water is added to the retort and the distillation is continued. After a month and a half of this (approximately), an earth has become manifest in the alchemist glass. As this process continues the quantity of material is multiplied. This process is called the flights of the eagles in alchemy which have been illuminated in this book. Once the desired amount of material is reached, the alchemist can switch to the multiplication of virtue.

To do this we simply begin adding the distillate back to the earth and continue the flights of the eagles. The matter is distilled, at this point the matter should have the appearance of a white wax type substance. The distilled water is poured back onto the earth. Alchemists repeated this second half of the white water stone process ten times being called ten flights of the eagles. Color changes in this work can be caused by distillation in metal apparatus, (alchemists used glass), or by what qualities are present in the water which reflects back on where and how the water was collected. Some pools of water with leaves have shown a peacock's tail myriad of colors floating upon the surface. The first set of rotations of the alchemist wheel are the multiplication in quantity which cause the water to be changed into "earth" (Hermes emerald tablet), The second set of distillations (flight of eagles) purifies the "earth" more with each turn of the alchemist wheel. Michael Sendivogius in the new chemical light suggests that in this work we must know where heat is used, and where cold is needed.

The coagulation is done in an evaporation dish set in the cold after the liquid has been condensed as a white water. Alchemist manuscripts suggested if we are to know how to proceed we must ask "GOD", suggesting that we must receive it as a gift from God or by the ocular demonstration of a teacher. By this they mean the red "stone". Which is prepared in the vessel of nature as outlined in this book, wherein nature herself has changed the water into wine and prepared it ready to the hand of those that know the secret. Father Christian Rosenkreutz, Christmas rosin salt.

THE MOON WAITS IN THE WATER BELOW.

ILLUMINATING THE HERMETIC MYSTERY

Alchemy And The Ravens Head

THE SECRET OF THE RED MERCURY

Steven School

DISSOLVING GOLD METAL IN THE BLOOD OF THE
GREEN LION.

CONDENSING AND COAGULATING MY ALCHEMICAL GREEN LION ACETATE. FROM IRON PYRITE USING WHITE VINEGAR AND PEROXIDE. DO NOT TRY THIS AT HOME.

DISSOLVING GOLD TURNED BLACK AND COLORED THE LIQUID WHICH SEEMS TO BE RECRYSTALLIZING IN HEAT. ALCHEMY OF STEVEN SCHOOL.
BIBLE QUOTE JOEL 2:31
The sun shall be turned to darkness, and the moon to blood, before the great and awesome day of the Lord comes.

THE WHITE PHASE OF THE MOON IN THE METAL
ACETATE WET PATH OF ALCHEMY BY
STEVEN SCHOOL.

SOWING THE SEED OF GOLD IN THE WHITE FOLIATED EARTH. METAL ACETATE PATH ALCHEMY OF STEVEN SCHOOL WITH IRON PYRITE AND PERACETIC ACID.

7 THE VESSEL OF NATURE

IN MEMORY OF FATHER CHRISTIAN ROSENKREUTZ

In the writings of Michael Sendivogius he describes the vessel of nature as being one, he calls it round, and even refers to it as "the circumference". He describes this, as something being thrust forth into the air. We shall proceed to the circulations in the vessel of nature. The alchemist may assist nature in setting the proper conditions in opening the golden branch, the golden bough. After we open the entrance to the closed palace naf the king, nature does the work without the laying on of hands. The matter is one, the vessel is one.

MICHAEL SENDIVOGIUS, THE NEW CHEMICAL LIGHT
ELEVENTH TREATISE.

Concerning the practical preparation of our Stone or Tincture by means of our Art

"When you observe at the bottom ashes of a brown color, while the water is almost red, you should open the vessel and dip a feather into it."

Christopher Columbus set sail for the new world and Ponce De Leon went searching for the legendary fountain of youth. As Christopher sailed the seas his men became sick. Soon they were afflicted with terrible symptoms seeming to indicate every type of sickness, disease, or plague was upon them like a curse. Eventually they reached land and deduced the cause of their health decline was attributed to a lack of vitamin C since they had no way to get fresh fruit during the voyage. They looked for a remedy in this strange new land, and behold! They discovered something which seemed to miraculously relieve even the worst of their ailments. Alchemist's like Nicholas Flamel indicated in their writings, the day a certain substance finally came over the helm, it was known by its distinct and pleasant aroma.

In the Emerald Tablets of Thoth Hermes from Atlantis, he illuminates to us a certain substance the wind hath carried in its belly. Water. If we study the countless circulations of nature in the earth's crust driven by the rain cycle, we see stalactites and stalagmites grow in the caverns of the earth, with the rise and fall of the water. But how do these repeated circulations affect things above ground in the realm of the vegetables? Perhaps the moisture on its upward ascent thrusts something forth from the earth's crust and continually propels it high into the air.

What Christopher Columbus discovered was probably shown to him by the natives who were already living here.

REVELATION 22 KJV.
In the midst of the street of it, and on either side of the river, was there the tree of life, which bare twelve manner of fruits, and yielded her fruit every month: and the leaves of the tree were for the healing of the nations.

Alchemist's liked to hide their secrets in the titles of their publications, in the colors and symbolism of their artwork, and even in their own name. The salt of the world, so carefully rectified by so many countless circulations in the vessel of nature.

The pine tree in the midst of the garden is the vessel of nature. The rings symbolize the countless circulations performed without the laying on of hands as the substance is being prepared by nature alone. The artist may assist by limbing the tree, so the substance may appear.
Alchemist's did like to hide their secrets and one alchemist in particular Father Christian Rosenkreutz of the famous chymical wedding comes to mind. Rosen and Kreutz, which means rosin salt.

Rosin is used in metallurgy as a fluxing agent. See rosin core solder. When pine trees are injured they begin to drip sap. At first it is often clear, then turns yellow, and finally it can become in appearance as a red crystal like a stone yet no stone. This water has been changed into earth by the place, which is the interior of the pine tree.

So Michael Sendivogius illuminated this tree as being thrust forth into the air, the "ashes" (tree bark) as brown, and the "water almost red" which is the dripping sap.   And Christopher Columbus found the pine needle tea. And Ponce De Leon found the vine of the wise bearing grapes.

A Work of Hermes. Not the same as alchemy with metals, or animal realm alchemy. The older simple methods of Hermes were illuminated in Michael Sendivogius New Chemical Light.

Life exists in the garden that was built for us. Death is the opposite of life. It is up to us to maintain this garden. If everyone would at least once in their life, travel deep into the forests of the world, The places where people do not usually go, and plant an apple tree, or a grape vine, a cherry tree etc, perhaps we could maintain or even improve the garden that was built for us. Let us turn the world into the food forest it was meant to be.

Michael Sendivogius, Alchemist. 1566 – 1636. Mentored by Alexander Seton.

Belle was a Mother, and a Grandmother. She lived 10 years, and 8 months. My friend died.

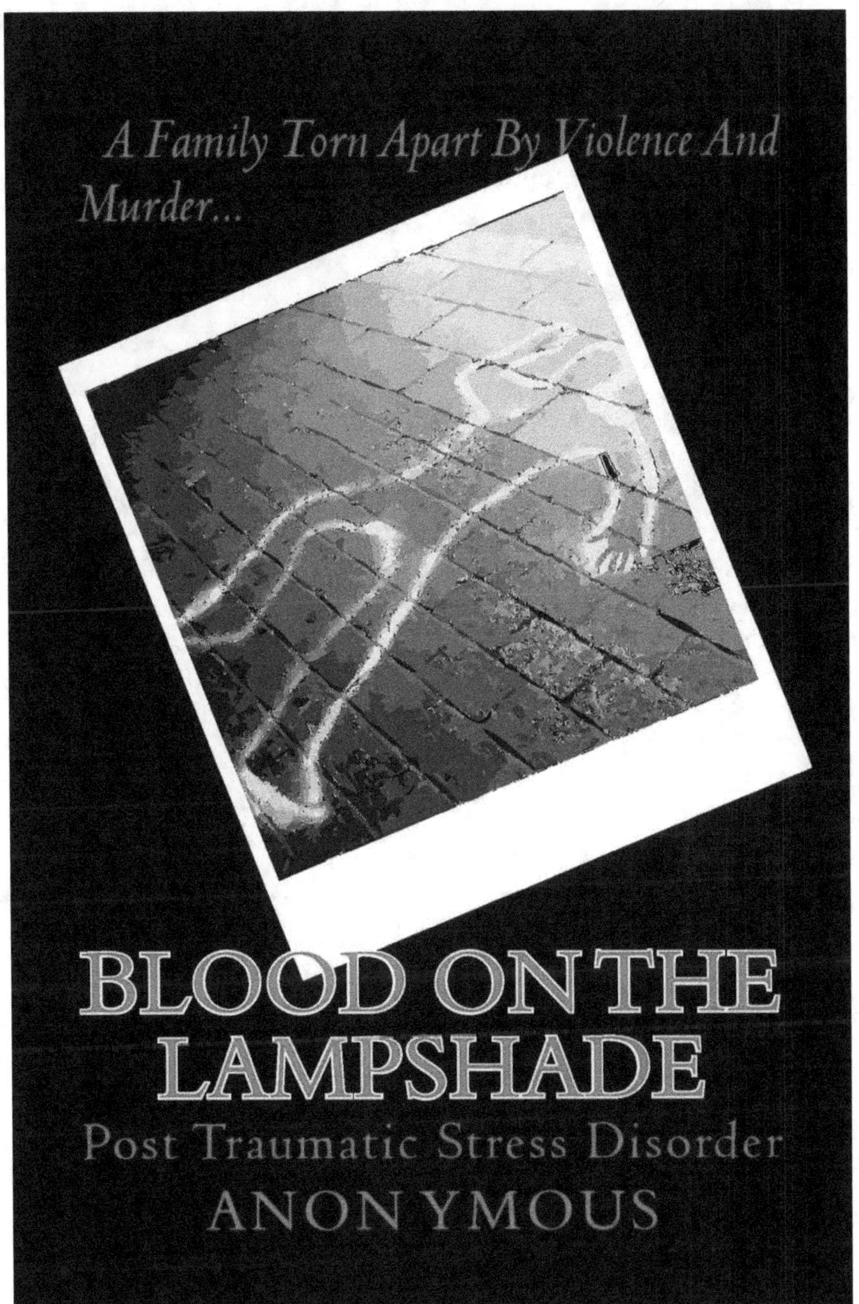

Blood on the lampshade

Blood On The Lampshade: Post Traumatic Stress Disorder
Paperback – July 17, 2018

The dream I had in the book, was a misunderstood premonition of the events that would unfold on February 19th, 2022.

As I walked along the fenced path adjacent to that big green field overlooking an ocean of eternity on the astral plane I approached a pen expecting to see Rico and expecting to make amends with him. Much to my surprise however it was Belle that emerged. She looked up into my eyes with both of us realizing what time it actually was. As I opened the second gate she looked up at me one last time as if to say goodbye to an old friend. Belle entered the spirit world with great dignity and courage. I remember this day with my friend.

ABOUT THE AUTHOR

The Philosopher's Stone has been on my mind since around 1987 when I saw a poem in my high school library about "A stone yet no stone",and it mentioned something about white, like wax. I have long since finally forgotten the exact words to that poem, however in 2008 I decided to seriously dig in to alchemy with research and experimentation. Alchemy can be a confusing subject, I have invested time trying to sort out what alchemy was, and how it works. The year now is 2023.
Steven School.

Let us finish with a quote from Michael Sendivogius New Chemical Light. "Let him consider that this mystery is for wise men, and not for fools".

64

Alchemy Books by Steven School are available on Amazon . Com